400+

Knock Knock Jokes

for Kids

Shanon Kasten

ISBN: 9798550186695

Comedy, humor, and joke-telling have many positive benefits associated with it. Jokes can bring a smile to the face of others and put you in a great mood!

CONTENTS

1   Name Jokes   5

2   Place Jokes   68

3   Holiday Jokes   75

4   Food Jokes   82

5   Animal Jokes   92

6   Object Jokes   98

7   More Knock-Knock Jokes   106

8   Bonus Jokes and Riddles   124

Name Jokes

Knock knock!

Who's there?

Beethoven!

Beethoven who?

Beethoven is too hot to touch!

Knock knock!

Who's there?

Abby!

Abby who?

Abby C D E F G!

Knock knock!

Who's there?

Buggy!

Buggy who?

This new app I downloaded is very buggy!

Knock knock!

Who's there?

Clark!

Clark who?

Clark your car in the garage!

Knock knock!

Who's there?

Claude!

Claude who?

Claude up by the cat!

Knock knock!

Who's there?

Jenny Linn!

Jenny Linn who?

Jenny Linn me some money please!

Knock knock!

Who's there?

Aileen!

Aileen who?

Aileen against the door until you open it!

Knock knock!

Who's there?

Noah!

Noah who?

Noah one will let me in!

Knock knock!

Who's there?

Aladdin!

Aladdin who?

Aladdin the street wants a word with you!

Knock knock!

Who's there?

Alba!

Alba who?

Alba in the kitchen if you need me!

Knock knock!

Who's there?

Coffin!

Coffin who?

Coffin and spluttering!

Knock knock!

Who's there?

Costa!

Costa who?

Costa lot!

Knock knock!

Who's there?

Clare!

Clare who?

Clare your throat before you speak!

Knock knock!

Who's there?

A Fred!

A Fred who?

Who's a Fred of the Big Bad Wolf?

Knock knock!

Who's there?

Baby owl!

Baby owl who?

Baby owl see you later!

Knock knock!

Who's there?

Albee!

Albee who?

Albee a monkey's uncle!

Knock knock!

Who's there?

Crete!

Crete who?

Crete to see you again!

Knock, knock.
Who's there?
Anita.
Anita who?
Anita borrow a pencil.

Knock, knock.
Who's there?
Dwayne.
Dwayne who?
**Dwayne the bathtub, it's
overflowing!**

Knock, knock.
Who's there?
Lena.
Lena who?
Lena little closer and I'll tell you.

Knock, knock.

Who's there?

Harry.

Harry who?

Harry up, it's cold out here!

Knock, knock.

Who's there?

William.

William who?

William mind your own business!

Knock, knock.

Who's there?

Noah.

Noah who?

Noah good place we can get something to eat?

Knock, knock.

Who's there?

Dora.

Dora who?

Dora's locked. That's why I'm knocking!

Knock, knock.

Who's there?

Howard.

Howard who?

Howard you?

Knock, knock.

Who's there?

Phillip.

Phillip who?

Phillip your pool. I wanna take a dip!

Knock, knock.

Who's there?

Jo.

Jo who?

Jo King!

Knock, knock.

Who's there?

Iva.

Iva who?

Iva sore hand from knocking.

Knock, knock.

Who's there?

Mikey.

Mikey who?

Mikey doesn't fit in the hole!

Knock, knock.

Who's there?

Kent.

Kent who?

Kent you tell by my voice?

Knock, knock.

Who's there?

Luke.

Luke who?

Luke through the peephole and find out!

Knock, knock.

Who's there?

Jess.

Jess who?

Jess me and my shadow!

Knock, knock.
Who's there?
Doris.
Doris who?
Doris locked, that's why I knocked!

Knock, knock.
Who's there?
Mae.
Mae who?
Mae be I'll tell you and Mae be I won't!

Knock, knock.
Who's there?
Sabina.
Sabina who?
Sabina long time since I've seen you!

Knock, knock.

Who's there?

Arfur.

Arfur who?

Arfur got!

Knock, knock.

Who's there?

Isabel.

Isabel who?

Isabel working? I had to knock!

Knock, knock.

Who's there?

Barbie.

Barbie who?

Barbie Q. Chicken!

Knock, knock.

Who's there?

Nana.

Nana who?

Nana your business!

Knock, knock.

Who's there?

Amy.

Amy who?

Amy 'fraid I've forgotten.

Knock, knock.

Who's there?

Justin.

Justin who?

Justin the neighborhood, thought I would drop by.

Knock, knock.

Who's there?

Ben.

Ben who?

Ben knocking for ten minutes!

Knock, knock.

Who's there?

Emma.

Emma who?

Emma bit cold out here, could you let me in?

Knock, knock.

Who's there?

Maya.

Maya who?

Maya name is Dan

Knock, knock.
Who's there?
Mia.
Mia who?
Mia and my shadow!

Knock, knock.
Who's there?
Gladys.
Gladys who?
Gladys the weekend, aren't you?

Knock, knock.
Who's there?
Greta.
Greta who?
You Greta on my nerves!

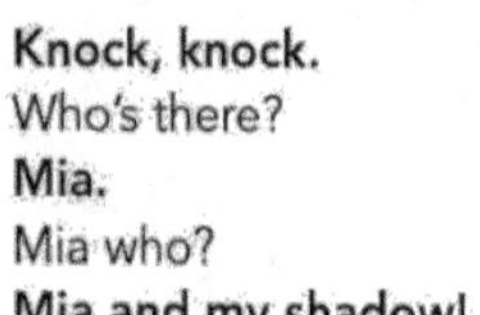

Knock, knock.

Who's there?

Dewey.

Dewey who?

Dewey have to keep telling silly jokes?

Knock, knock.

Who's there?

Mary Lee.

Mary Lee who?

Mary Lee, Mary Lee, Mary Lee, Mary Lee, life is but a dream!

Knock, knock.

Who's there?

Abe.

Abe who?

Abe C D E F G . . .

Knock, knock.

Who's there?

Ivana.

Ivana who?

Ivana come in!

Knock, knock.

Who's there?

Carl.

Carl who?

Carl get you there faster than a bike!

Knock, knock.

Who's there?

Norma Lee.

Norma Lee who?

Norma Lee I don't go around knocking on doors, but I just had to meet you!

Knock, knock.

Who's there?

Oswald.

Oswald who?

Oswald my bubblegum.

Knock, knock.

Who's there?

Adam.

Adam who?

Adam my way, I'm coming through!

Knock, knock.

Who's there?

Olive.

Olive who?

Olive right next door.

Knock, knock.

Who's there?

Otto.

Otto who?

Otto know. I've got amnesia.

Knock, knock.

Who's there?

Scott.

Scott who?

Scott nothing to do with you!

Knock, knock.

Who's there?

Ida.

Ida who?

Ida like to be your friend!

Knock, knock.

Who's there?

Howard.

Howard who?

Howard you know unless you open the door?

Knock, knock.

Who's there?

Sacha.

Sacha who?

Sacha lot of questions.

Knock, knock.

Who's there?

Wanda.

Wanda who?

Wanda buy some Girl Scout cookies?

Knock, knock.

Who's there?

Brad.

Brad who?

I've got Brad news, I'm afraid!

Knock, knock.

Who's there?

Abbott.

Abbott who?

Abbott time you opened this door!

Knock, knock.

Who's there?

Frank.

Frank who?

Frank you for being my friend.

Knock, knock.

Who's there?

Isaiah.

Isaiah who?

Isaiah nothing until you open this door!

Knock, knock.

Who's there?

Ali.

Ali who?

Ali wanna do is have some fun.

Knock, knock.

Who's there?

Shelby.

Shelby who?
Shelby coming around the mountain when she comes.
Shelby coming around the mountain when she comes.
Shelby coming around the mountain. Shelby coming
around the mountain when she comes!

Knock, knock.

Who's there?

Dawn.

Dawn who?

Dawn leave me out in the cold!

Knock, knock.

Who's there?

Omar.

Omar who?

Omar goodness! This is the wrong door!

Knock, knock.

Who's there?

Alma.

Alma who?

Alma not going to tell you.

Knock, knock.

Who's there?

Avery.

Avery who?

Avery time I come to your house we go through this again!

Knock, knock.

Who's there?

Sam.

Sam who?

Sam day you'll recognize me.

Knock, knock.

Who's there?

Sara.

Sara who?

Sara 'nother way in?

Knock, knock.

Who's there?

Elias.

Oh, hi, Elias, come in, come in.

You're supposed to say, "Elias who?"

Knock, knock.

Who's there?

Shirley.

Shirley who?

Shirley you must know me by now!

Knock, knock.

Who's there?

Benny.

Benny who?

Benny thing happening with you today?

Knock, knock.

Who's there?

Al.

Al who?

Al give you a hug if you let me in!

Knock, knock.
Who's there?
Althea.
Althea who?
Althea later alligator!

Knock, knock.
Who's there?
Denise.
Denise who?
Denise are above the ankles.

Knock, knock.
Who's there?
Maura.
Maura who?
Maura the merrier!

Knock, knock.

Who's there?

Simon.

Simon who?

Simon the other side of the door. If you opened up, you'd see!

Knock, knock.

Who's there?

Juno.

Juno who?

Juno who it is!

Knock, knock.

Who's there?

Sloane.

Sloane who?

Sloanely outside. Let me in!

Knock, knock.

Who's there?

Theodore.

Theodore who?

Theodore was locked so I knocked!

Knock, knock.

Who's there?

Abbey.

Abbey who?

Abbey stung me on the nose!

Knock, knock.

Who's there?

Manuel.

Manuel who?

Manuel be sorry if you don't answer this door!

Knock, knock.

Who's there?

Isaiah.

Isaiah who?

Isaiah 'gain, knock, knock!

Knock, knock.

Who's there?

Annie.

Annie who?

Annie body home?

Knock, knock.

Who's there?

Barry.

Barry who?

Barry nice to see you!

Knock, knock.

Who's there?

Pete.

Pete who?

Pete-za delivery!

Knock, knock.

Who's there?

Marie.

Marie who?

Marie me? I love you!

Knock, knock.

Who's there?

Ewan.

Ewan who?

No, it's just me!

Knock, knock.

Who's there?

Danielle.

Danielle who?

Danielle so loud! I heard you the first time!

Knock, knock.

Who's there?

Rita.

Rita who?

Rita book, you might learn something!

Knock, knock.

Who's there?

Justin.

Justin who?

Justin time for dinner!

Knock, knock.

Who's there?

Max.

Max who?

Max no difference!

Knock, knock.

Who's there?

Ivan.

Ivan who?

Ivan idea you know who it is!

Knock, knock.

Who's there?

Uriah.

Uriah who?

Keep uriah on the ball!

Knock, knock.

Who's there?

Hal.

Hal who?

Halloo to you too!

Knock, knock.

Who's there?

Haman.

Haman who?

Haman! It's cold out here!

Knock, knock.

Who's there?

Meg.

Meg who?

Meg up your mind! Are you going to let me in or not?

Knock, knock.

Who's there?

Mickey.

Mickey who?

Mickey is lost! That's why I'm knocking!

Knock, knock.

Who's there?

Howard.

Howard who?

Howard can it be to guess a knock-knock joke?

Knock, knock.

Who's there?

Mischa.

Mischa who?

I Mischa a lot!

Knock, knock.

Who's there?

Les.

Les who?

Les go out and play.

Knock, knock.

Who's there?

Luke.

Luke who?

Luke through the peephole and find out.

Knock, knock.

Who's there?

Ida.

Ida who?

Ida know. Sorry!

Knock, knock.

Who's there?

Linda.

Linda who?

Linda hand! I can't do it all by myself!

Knock, knock.

Who's there?

Ken.

Ken who?

Ken you open the door and let me in?

Knock, knock.

Who's there?

Owen.

Owen who?

Owen are you going to let me in?

Knock, knock.

Who's there?

Nadia.

Nadia who?

Nadia head if you understand me.

Knock, knock.

Who's there?

Stan.

Stan who?

Stan back! I'm knocking this door down!

Knock, knock.

Who's there?

Juan.

Juan who?

Juan to hear some more of these knock knock jokes?

Knock knock!

Who's there?

Adam!

Adam who?

Adam up and tell me the total!

Knock knock!

Who's there?

Adelia!

Adelia who?

Adelia the cards after you cut the deck!

Knock knock!

Who's there?

Adeline!

Adeline who?

Adeline extra to the letter!

Knock knock!

Who's there?

Adolf!

Adolf who?

Adolf ball hit me in the mouth!

Knock knock!

Who's there?

Burglar!

Burglar who?

Burglars don't knock!

Knock knock!

Who's there?

Abbey!

Abbey who?

Abbey stung me on the nose!

Knock knock!

Who's there?

Aaron!

Aaron who?

Aaron the barber's floor!

Knock knock!

Who's there?

Underwear!

Underwear who?

Underwear my baby is tonight?

Knock knock!

Who's there?

Chuck!

Chuck who?

Chuck in a sandwich for lunch!

Knock knock!

Who's there?

Acid!

Acid who?

Accidently on purpose!

Knock knock!

Who's there?

Comic!

Comic who?

Comic and see me sometime!

Knock knock!

Who's there?

Cologne!

Cologne who?

Cologne me names won't help!

Knock knock!

Who's there?

Acis!

Acis who?

Acis spades!

Knock knock!

Who's there?

Ada!

Ada who?

A diamond is forever!

Knock knock!

Who's there?

Adair!

Adair who?

Adair once but now I'm bald now!

Knock knock!

Who's there?

Bacon!

Bacon who?

Bacon a cake for your birthday!

Knock knock!

Who's there?

Cindy!

Cindy who?

Cindy next one in please!

Knock knock!

Who's there?

Ahmed!

Ahmed who?

Ahmed a big mistake coming here!

Knock knock!

Who's there?

Boo!

Boo who?

Don't cry. It's just a joke!

Knock knock!

Who's there?

Abel!

Abel who?

Abel to see you if you open up!

Knock knock!

Who's there?

Cereal!

Cereal who?

Cereal pleasure to finally meet you!

Knock knock!

Who's there?

Albert!

Albert who!

Albert you don't know who this is!

Knock knock!

Who's there?

Aldo!

Aldo who?

Aldo anywhere with you!

Knock knock!

Who's there?

Aitch!

Aitch who?

Bless You!

Knock knock!

Who's there?

Neil!

Neil who?

Neil down to your leader!

Knock knock!

Who's there?

Althea!

Althea who?

Althea when you open the door!

Knock knock!

Who's there?

May!

May who?

May I come in?

Knock knock!

Who's there?

Alf!

Alf who?

I pay Alf the rent here. Let me in!

Knock knock!

Who's there?

Ocelot!

Ocelot who?

You Ocelot of questions, don't you?

Knock knock!

Who's there?

Agatha!

Agatha who?

Agatha headache. Do you have an aspirin?

Knock knock!

Who's there?

Agent!

Agent who?

Agentle breeze!

Knock knock!

Who's there?

Keri!

Keri who?

Keri out the trash!

Knock knock!

Who's there?

Coda!

Coda who?

Coda paint!

Knock knock!

Who's there?

Alec!

Alec who?

Alec-tricity. Isn't that a shock!

Knock knock!

Who's there?

Alma!

Alma who?

Knock knock!

Who's there?

Manny!

Manny who?

Manny times I have knocked on this door!

Knock knock!

Who's there?

Alligator!

Alligator who?

Alligator for his birthday was a card!

Knock knock!

Who's there?

Yucca!

Yucca who?

Yucca open the door and find out!

Knock knock!

Who's there?

Aleta!

Aleta who?

Aleta from the bill man!

Knock knock!

Who's there?

Alpaca!

Alpaca who?

Alpaca lunch for us to eat later!

Knock knock!

Who's there?

Alfred!

Alfred who!

Alfred of the dog! Open the door!

Knock knock!

Who's there?

Ina!

Ina who?

Ina get in this house sooner or later!

Knock knock!

Who's there?

Hugo!

Hugo who?

Hugo first!

Knock knock!

Who's there?

Caitlin!

Caitlin who?

Caitlin you my shoes. I'm wearing them today!

Knock knock!

Who's there?

Toby!

Toby who?

Toby or not to be? That is the question.

Knock knock!

Who's there?

Nunya!

Nunya who?

Nunya business!

Knock knock!

Who's there?

Juno!

Juno who?

Juno how long I've been knocking on this door?

Knock knock!

Who's there?

Yule!

Yule who?

Yule never guess!

Knock knock!

Who's there?

Icy!

Icy who?

Icy you! Let me in!

Knock knock!

Who's there?

Alex Plane!

Alex Plane who?

Alex Plane the details later!

Knock knock!

Who's there?

Bull!

Bull who?

Bull the door closed when you come in!

Knock knock!

Who's there?

Alka!

Alka who?

Alka pone!

Knock knock!

Who's there?

Alexander!

Alexander who?

Alexander friend are coming over soon!

Knock knock!

Who's there?

Tennessee!

Tennessee who?

You're the only Tennessee tonight!

Knock knock!

Who's there?

Alda!

Alda who?

Alda time you knew who it was!

Knock knock!

Who's there?

Alexia!

Alexia who?

Alexia again to open this door right now!

Knock knock!

Who's there?

Bass!

Bass who?

Bass the salt please!

Knock knock!

Who's there?

Allison!

Allison who?

Allison to you if you will listen to me!

Knock knock!

Who's there?

Bobby!

Bobby who?

Bobby for apples at the birthday party!

Knock knock!

Who's there?

Mabel!

Mabel who?

You can have Mabel syrup on your pancakes!

Knock knock!

Who's there?

Olive!

Olive who?

Knock knock!

Who's there?

Toucan!

Toucan who?

Toucan open up this door!

Knock knock!

Who's there?

Bassoon!

Bassoon who?

Bassoon things will get better!

Knock knock!

Who's there?

Al!

Al who?

Al lied!

Place Jokes

Knock, knock.

Who's there?
Utah.
Utah who?
Utah-king to me?

Knock, knock.

Who's there?
Europe.
Europe who?
Europe to no good!

Knock, knock.

Who's there?
Ohio.
Ohio who?
Oh, hi, how are you doing?

Knock, knock.

Who's there?
Venice.
Venice who?
Venice your mother coming home?

Knock, knock.

Who's there?
Babylon.
Babylon who?
Babylon. I'm not really listening.

Knock, knock.

Who's there?
Russian.
Russian who?
Stop Russian me!

Knock, knock.

Who's there?
Alaska.
Alaska who?
Alaska 'nother person if you don't know the answer.

Knock, knock.

Who's there?
Guinea.
Guinea who?
Guinea high five!

Knock, knock.

Who's there?
Avenue.
Avenue who?
Avenue heard this joke before?

Knock, knock.

Who's there?
Indonesia.
Indonesia who?
I see you and I get weak Indonesia!

Knock, knock.

Who's there?
Sodom.
Sodom who?
Sodom earlier, but didn't talk to them.

Knock, knock.

Who's there?
Norway.
Norway who?
Norway will I leave until you open this door!

Knock, knock.

Who's there?
Chile.
Chile who?
It's getting Chile out here, let me in!

Knock, knock.

Who's there?
Uruguay.
Uruguay who?
You go Uruguay and I'll go mine!

Knock, knock.

Who's there?
Heaven.
Heaven who?
Heaven seen you in a while.

Knock, knock.

Who's there?
Germany.
Germany who?
Germany people knock on your door?

Knock, knock.

Who's there?
Aisle.
Aisle who?
Aisle see you around!

Knock, knock.

Who's there?
Juneau.
Juneau who?
Juneau what time it is?

Knock knock!

Who's there?
Alaska!
Alaska who?
Alaska my parents if I can go!

Knock knock!

Who's there?
Jamaica!
Jamaica who?
Jamaica mistake if you don't open up!

Knock knock!

Who's there?

Bosnia!

Bosnia who?

Bosnia bell on this door last time?

Knock knock!

Who's there?

Texas!

Texas who?

Texas are rising every year!

Knock, knock.
Who's there?
Iran.
Iran who?
Iran all the way over here to tell you
something.

Knock, knock.
Who's there?
Area.
Area who?
Area there? It's me!

Knock, knock.
Who's there?
Jamaica.
Jamaica who?
Jamaica great friend!

Holiday Jokes

Knock, knock.

Who's there?
Twig.
Twig who?
Twig or tweat!

Knock, knock.

Who's there?
Murray.
Murray who?
Murray Christmas to all and to all a good night!

Knock, knock.

Who's there?
Snow.
Snow who?
Snow one is gonna open the door.

Knock, knock.

Who's there?
Witch.
Witch who?
Witch one of you can fix my broomstick?

Knock, knock.
Who's there?
Sherwood.
Sherwood who?
Sherwood like to be your Valentine!

Knock, knock.
Who's there?
Adore.
Adore who?
Adore is between us. Open up!

Knock, knock.
Who's there?
Osborn.
Osborn who?
Osborn today—it's my birthday!

Knock, knock.

Who's there?
Avery.
Avery who?
Avery merry Christmas to you!

Knock, knock.

Who's there?
Yule.
Yule who?
Yule never know!

Knock, knock.

Who's there?
Snow.
Snow who?
Snow business of yours!

Knock, knock.

Who's there?
Icy.
Icy who?
Icy you in there! Open the door!

Knock, knock.

Who's there?
Abby.
Abby who?
Abby birthday to you!

Knock, knock.

Who's there?
Irish.
Irish who?
Irish you a Merry Christmas!

Knock, knock.

Who's there?
Sandy.
Sandy who?
Sandy Claus!

Knock, knock.

Who's there?
Howl.
Howl who?
Howl you be dressing up for Halloween this year?

Knock, knock.

Who's there?
Dexter.
Dexter who?
Dexter halls with boughs of holly!

Knock, knock.

Who's there?
Phillip.
Phillip who?
Phillip my bag with Halloween candy!

Knock, knock.

Who's there?
Wanda.
Wanda who?
Wanda wish you a happy birthday!

Knock, knock.

Who's there?
Hannah.
Hannah who?
Hannah partridge in a pear tree.

Knock, knock.

Who's there?
Value.
Value who?
Value be my Valentine?

Knock, knock.

Who's there?
 Snow.
Snow who?
Snow use, I forgot my name!

Knock, knock.

Who's there?
Mary and Abby.
Mary and Abby who?
Mary Christmas and Abby New Year!

Knock, knock.

Who's there?
Boo.
Boo who?
Don't cry—it's just a knock-knock joke.

Knock knock!

Who's there?

Conga!

Conga who?

Conga on standing outside all day!

Food Jokes

Knock, knock.

Who's there?
Honeydew.
Honeydew who?
Honeydew you want to hear a knock knock joke?

Knock, knock.

Who's there?
Orange.
Orange who?
Orange you going to let me in?

Knock, knock.

Who's there?
Doughnut.
Doughnut who?
Doughnut ask, it's a secret!

Knock, knock.

Who's there?
Lettuce.
Lettuce who?
Lettuce in, it's cold out here!

Knock, knock.

Who's there?
Beets.
Beets who?
Beets me!

Knock, knock.

Who's there?
Kiwi.
Kiwi who?
Kiwi go to the store?

Knock, knock.

Who's there?
Cash.
Cash who?
I knew you were a nut!

Knock, knock.

Who's there?
Ice cream.
Ice cream who?
Ice cream if you don't let me in!

Knock, knock.

Who's there?
Turnip.
Turnip who?
Turnip the volume, it's too quiet.

Knock, knock.

Who's there?
Ketchup.
Ketchup who?
Ketchup with you soon!

Knock, knock.

Who's there?
Beef.
Beef who?
Beef-or I get cold, you'd better let me in!

Knock, knock.

Who's there?
Cook.
Cook who?
Hey! Who you calling cuckoo?

Knock, knock.

Who's there?
Bean.
Bean who?
Bean a while since I saw you last!

Knock, knock.

Who's there?
Broccoli.
Broccoli who?
Broccoli doesn't have a last name, silly!

Knock, knock.

Who's there?
Water.
Water who?
Water way to answer the door!

Knock, knock.

Who's there?
Omelet.
Omelet who?
Omelet smarter than I look.

Knock, knock.
Who's there?
Bean.
Bean who?
Bean fishing lately?

Knock, knock.
Who's there?
Figs.
Figs who?
Figs the doorbell, it's broken!

Knock, knock.
Who's there?
Aida.
Aida who?
**Aida sandwich for lunch today.
Do you want one?**

Knock, knock.

Who's there?
You be.
You be who?
You be a pal and bring me a cookie!

Knock, knock.

Who's there?
Orange juice.
Orange juice who?
Orange juice going to invite me in?

Knock, knock.

Who's there?
 Butter.
Butter who?
It's butter if you don't know!

Knock, knock.

Who's there?
Doughnut.
Doughnut who?
Doughnut be afraid, it's just me!

Knock, knock.

Who's there?
Peas.
Peas who?
Peas open the door for me!

Knock, knock.

Who's there?
Water.
Water who?
Water you doing?

Knock, knock.

Who's there?
Banana.
Banana who?

Knock, knock.
Who's there?
Orange.
Orange who?
Orange you glad I didn't say banana?

Knock knock!

Who's there?
Oil!
Oil who?
Oil beat you up if you don't open the door!

Knock knock!

Who's there?
Cookie!
Cookie who?
Cookie quit and now I have to make all the food!

Knock knock!

Who's there?
Cole!
Cole who?
Cole as a cucumber!

Knock, knock.
Who's there?
Cereal.
Cereal who?
Cereal pleasure to meet you!

Animal Jokes

Knock, knock.

Who's there?
Rhino.
Rhino who?
Rhino every knock knock joke there is!

Knock, knock.

Who's there?
Honeybee.
Honeybee who?
Honeybee a dear and open the door.

Knock, knock.

Who's there?
Alpaca.
Alpaca who?
Alpaca the trunk, you pack the suitcase.

Knock, knock.

Who's there?
A herd.
A herd who?
A herd you were home, so I came over!

Knock, knock.

Who's there?
Gorilla.
Gorilla who?
Gorilla me a steak, I'm hungry!

Dog: Tell me a joke.

Boy: You don't understand human jokes.
Dog: Why? Because humans are so much smarter
than dogs?

Boy: **Knock, knock.**

Dog: Hold on! There's someone at the door!
Be right back to hear the joke after I go see who's there!

Knock, knock.

Who's there?
Cowsgo.
Cowsgo who?
No, they don't. Cowsgo moo!

Knock, knock.

Who's there?
Bat.
Bat who?
Bat you'll never guess!

Knock, knock.

Who's there?
Kanga.
Kanga who?
No, kanga roo!

Knock, knock.

Who's there?
Howl.
Howl who?
Howl you know if you don't open the door?

Knock, knock.

Who's there?
Giraffe.
Giraffe who?
Giraffe anything to eat, I'm starving!

Knock, knock.

Who's there?
Aurora
Aurora who?
Aurora just came from a polar bear!

Knock, knock.

Who's there?
Meow.
Meow who?
Take meow to the ball game!

Knock, knock.

Who's there?
 Owls.
Owls who?
That's right, owls whoooooooooo!

Knock, knock.

Who's there?
Lion.
Lion who?
Lion on your doorstep, open up!

Knock, knock.

Who's there?
Amos.
Amos who?
Amos-quito!

Knock, knock.

Who's there?
Anudder.
Anudder who?
Anudder mosquito!

Knock, knock.

Who's there?
Goat.
Goat who?
Goat to the door and find out!

Knock, knock.

Who's there?
Crab.
Crab who?
Crab me a snack, please!

Knock, knock.

Who's there?
Interrupting cow.
Interrupting c—
Mooooo!

Knock, knock.

Who's there?
Cook.
Cook who?
Stop making bird noises and open the door!

Knock, knock.

Who's there?
Beehive.
Beehive who?
Beehive yourself!

Knock, knock.

Who's there?
Iguana.
Iguana who?
Iguana tell you another knock knock joke!

Knock knock!

Who's there?
Cows!
Cows who?
Cows go moo not who!

Knock, knock.
Who's there?
Beaver.
Beaver who?
Beaver-y quiet and no one will hear us!

Knock, knock.
Who's there?
Toucan.
Toucan who?
Toucan play that game!

Knock, knock.
Who's there?
Wood ant.
Wood ant who?
Don't be afraid. I wood ant hurt a fly!

Object Jokes

Knock, knock

Who's there?
Radio.
Radio who?
Radio not, here I come!

Knock, knock.

Who's there?
Canoe.
Canoe who?
Canoe come over and play?

Knock, knock.

Who's there?
Wooden shoe.
Wooden shoe who?
Wooden shoe like to know?

Knock, knock.

Who's there?
I eat mop.
I eat mop who?
You do what??

Knock, knock.

Who's there?
Dishes.
Dishes who?
Dishes me, who are you?

Knock, knock.

Who's there?
Cargo.
Cargo who?
Cargo "beep, beep, vroom, vroom!"

Knock, knock.

Who's there?
Juicy.
Juicy who?
Juicy my set of keys?

Knock, knock.

Who's there?
Needle.
Needle who?
Needle little money for the movies!

Knock, knock.

Who's there?
One shoe.
One shoe who?
One shoe play with me?

Knock, knock.

Who's there?
A broken pencil.
A broken pencil who?
Never mind. It's pointless!

Knock, knock.

Who's there?
Dishes.
Dishes who?
Dishes the FBI, open up!

Knock, knock.

Who's there?
Fiddle.
Fiddle who?
Fiddle make you happy, I'll tell you!

Knock, knock.

Who's there?
Dishes.
Dishes who?
Dishes a nice place!

Knock, knock.

Who's there?
Wooden shoe.
Wooden shoe who?
Wooden shoe like to hear another joke?

Knock knock!

Who's there?
Back!
Bach who?
Back to work!

Knock knock!

Who's there?
Curry!
Curry who?
Curry me back home will you!?

Knock knock!

Who's there?
Curly!
Curly who?
Curly Q!

Knock knock!

Who's there?
C's!
C's who?
C's the day!

Knock knock!

Who's there?
Crock and dial!
Crock and dial who?
Crock and dial Dundee!

Knock knock!

Who's there?
Adore!
Adore who?
Adore stands between us, open up!

Knock knock!

Who's there?
Banana!
Banana who?
Banana split so ice creamed!

Knock knock!

Who's there?
Closure!
Closure who?
Closure mouth when you eat!

Knock knock!

Who's there?
Cook!
Cook who?
Cuckoo yourself, I don't come here to be insulted!

Knock knock!

Who's there?
Cotton!
Cotton who?
Cotton a trap!

Knock knock!

Who's there?

Cod!

Cod who?

Cod red-handed!

Knock knock!

Who's there?

Colin!

Colin who?

I'm Colin Mom if you do not open the door!

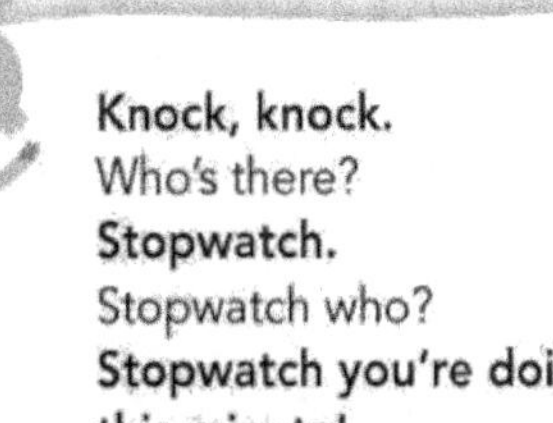

Knock, knock.
Who's there?
Stopwatch.
Stopwatch who?
Stopwatch you're doing right this minute!

Knock, knock.
Who's there?
Razor.
Razor who?
Razor hands in the air like you just don't care!

Knock, knock.
Who's there?
Train.
Train who?
Someone needs to train ya to open the door!

More Knock Knock Jokes

Knock, knock.

Who's there?
Yah!
Yah who?
Did I just hear a cowboy in there?

Knock, knock.

Who's there?
Mustache.
Mustache who?
Please let me in. I mustache you a question!

Knock, knock.

Who's there?
Weevil.
Weevil who?
Weevil only be staying a minute.

Knock, knock.

Who's there?
Says.
Says who?
Says me, that's who!

Knock, knock.

Who's there?
Ear.
Ear who?
Ear you are! I've been looking for you!

Knock, knock.

Who's there?
Sing.
Sing who?
Whooooooo!

Knock, knock.

It's open!

Knock, knock.
Who's there?
Knock.
Knock who?
Knock Knock!
Who's there?
Knock.
Knock who?
Knock Knock!
Who's there?
Knock.
Knock who?
Knock Knock!
Who's there?
Knock.
Knock who?
Knock Knock!
. . . . Ok, well come on in then.

Knock, knock.

Who's there?
Bingo.
Bingo who?
Bingo'ng to come see you for ages?

Knock, knock.

Who's there?
I   am.
I   am who?
You mean you don't remember who you are?

Knock, knock.

Who's there?
Ears.
Ears who?
Ears some more knock knock jokes for you!

Knock, knock.

Who's there?
Bless.
Bless who?
I didn't sneeze!

Knock, knock.

Who's there?
Dots.
Dots who?
Dots for me to know and you to find out!

Knock, knock.

Who's there?
Winner.
Winner who?
Winner you going to let me in?

Knock, knock.

Who's there?
Scold.
Scold who?
Scold outside!

Knock, knock.

Who's there?
Hebrews.
Hebrews who?
Hebrews some good coffee.

Will you remember me in a minute?

Yes.
Will you remember me in an hour?
Yes.
Will you remember me in a day?
Yes.
Will you remember me in a week?
Yes.
Will you remember me forever?
Yes.

Knock, knock.

Who's there?
You didn't remember me!

Knock, knock.

Who's there?
You know.
You know who?
Ah. It's You-know-who!

Knock, knock.

Who's there?
Hoover.
Hoover who?
Hoover you expecting?

Knock, knock.
Who's there?
Leaf.
Leaf who?
Leaf me alone!

Knock, knock.
Who's there?
Diploma.
Diploma who?
Diploma is here to fix the sink.

Knock, knock.
Who's there?
Repeat.
Repeat who?
Who, who, who, who, who.
How long do I have to do this?

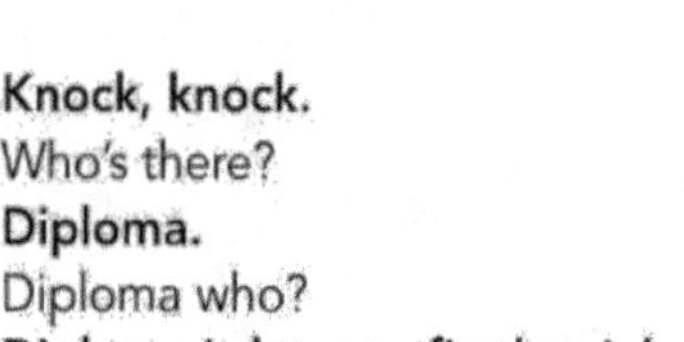

Knock, knock.

Who's there?
Yukon.
Yukon who?
Yukon say that again!

Knock, knock.

Who's there?
Nobel.
Nobel who?
No bell, that's why I knocked!

Knock, knock.

Who's there?
Disguise.
Disguise who?
Disguise your best friend!

Knock, knock.

Who's there?
Freeze
Freeze Who?
Freeze a Jolly Good Fellow!
Freeze a Jolly Good Fellow!
Freeze a Jolly Good Fellow!
Which nobody can deny!

Knock, knock.

Who's there?
Usher.
Usher who?
Usher wish you would let me in!

Knock, knock.

Who's there?
Churchill.
Churchill who?
Churchill be held on Sunday!

Knock, knock.

Who's there?
Icon.
Icon who?
Icon tell you another knock knock joke if you want!

Knock, knock.

Who's there?
Argue.
Argue who?
Argue going to let me in?

Knock, knock.

Who's there?
Summertime.
Summertime who?
Summertime you can be a big pest!

Knock, knock.
Who's there?
Knee.
Knee who?
Knee-d you ask?

Knock, knock.
Who's there?
Dozen.
Dozen who?
Dozen anybody want to let me in?

Knock, knock.
Who's there?
A little old lady.
A little old lady who?
I didn't know you could yodel!

Knock, knock.

Who's there?
Bashful.
Bashful who?
I can't say, I'm too embarrassed!

Knock, knock.

Who's there?
Passion.
Passion who?
Passion through and thought I'd come say hello!

Knock, knock.

Who's there?
Woo.
Woo who?
Don't get so excited, it's just a joke!

Knock, knock.

Who's there?
Hatch.
Hatch who?
God bless you!

Knock, knock.

Who's there?
Hacienda.
Hacienda who?
Hacienda the joke!

Knock, knock.

Who's there?
Issue.
Issue who?
Issue blind? It's me!

Knock, knock.

Who's there?
Ratio.
Ratio who?
Ratio to the end of the street!

Knock, knock.

Who's there?
Hominy.
Hominy who?
Hominy times are we going to have to go through
this?

Knock, knock.

Who's there?
Police.
Police who?
Police hurry up, it's chilly outside!

Knock, knock.

Who's there?
Knock, knock.
Who's there?
You're supposed to say "knock knock who!"

Knock, knock.

Who's there?
Impatient pirate.
Impatient p—
ARRRRRRRRRR!

Knock, knock.
Who's there?
Handsome.
Handsome who?
**Handsome money through the
keyhole and I'll tell you!**

Knock, knock.
Who's there?
Champ.
Champ who?
Champ poo your hair—it's dirty!

Knock, knock.
Who's there?
Tiss.
Tiss who?
**Tiss who is good for
blowing your nose!**

Knock, knock.

Who's there?
Zany.
Zany who?
Zany body home?

Knock, knock.

Who's there?
Waddle.
Waddle who?
Waddle you give me if I go away?

Knock, knock.

Who's there?
Spell.
Spell who?
W-H-O

Knock, knock.

Who's there?
Ya.
Ya who?
Wow. You sure are excited to see me!

Knock, knock

Who's there?
Voodoo.
Voodoo who?
Voodoo you think you are!

Knock, knock.

Who's there?

Doorbell repairman!
Doorbell repairman who?
Ding dong! My work here is done.

Knock, knock.

Who's there?
Opportunity.
Opportunity who?
Opportunity doesn't knock twice!

Bonus Jokes and Riddles

What happens to a frog's car when it breaks down?

It gets toad away.

What did the duck say when he bought lipstick?

"Put it on my bill."

Why was 6 afraid of 7?

Because 7, 8, 9.

What musical instrument is found in the bathroom?

A tuba toothpaste.

What do elves learn in school?

The elf-abet.

Why did the boy bring a ladder to school?

He wanted to go to high school.

Where do pencils go for vacation?

Pencil-vania.

Why did the girl smear peanut butter on the road?

To go with the traffic jam!

Why do bananas have to put on sunscreen before they go to the beach?

Because they might peel.

How do you make a tissue dance?

You put a little boogie in it.

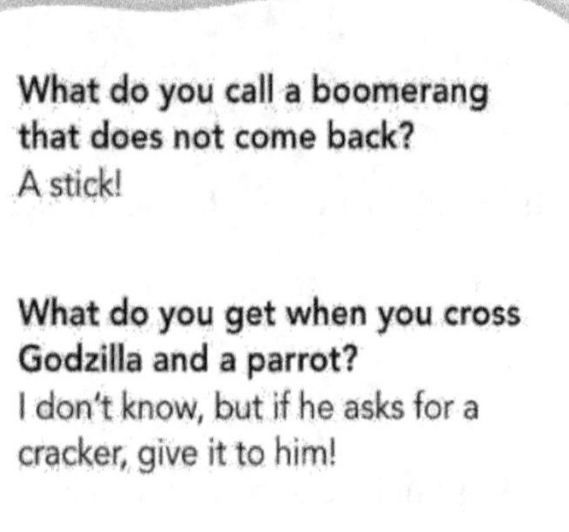

Which flower talks the most?

Tulips, of course, because they have two lips!

A man arrived in a small town on Friday. He stayed for two days and left on Friday. How is this possible?

His horse's name is Friday!

What did 0 say to 8?

Nice belt!

What did the mushroom say to the fungus?

You're a fun guy [fungi].

Why couldn't the pony sing himself a lullaby?

He was a little hoarse.

What do you get if you cross a parrot with a shark?

A bird that will talk your ear off.

What do you get when you cross a ghost and a cat?

A scaredy cat!

What do you get when you cross a fish and drumsticks?

Fish sticks.

What do you get when you cross a tiger and a blizzard?

Frostbite!

What do you get when you cross a fish with an elephant?

Swimming trunks.

What do you get when you cross a piece of paper and scissors?

Confetti.

What do you get when you cross a cow and a lawnmower?

A lawn-moo-er.

What do you get when you cross a cow with a trampoline?

A milkshake!

What do you call a cat crossed with a fish?

Catfish.

What do you get if you cross a fridge and a stereo?

Cool music!

What do you get if you cross a kangaroo and a snake?

A jump rope!

What do you get when you cross a karate expert with a pig?

A pork chop.

What do you get when you cross a chicken and a chihuahua?

Pooched eggs.

What do you get when you cross a lemon and a cat?

A sourpuss.

What do you call a race car that can't race?

A car.

What does lightning wear under their pants?

Thunderwear.

Why did the boy tiptoe in front of the medicine cabinet?

He didn't want to wake the sleeping pills.

What do you call a deer with no eyes?

No eye deer (no idea)

What do you call a cow that just had a baby?

De-calf-inated.

What do you call cows that are laying down?

Ground beef.

Why did the fastest cat in school get suspended?

Cuz he was a cheetah.

What does a piece of toast wear to bed?

His pa-JAM-as.

What do you call a dinosaur that does not take a bath?

A Stink-o-Saurus.

Why do fish live in salt water?

Because pepper makes them sneeze!

Why did the orange lose the race?

Because he ran out of juice.

Two muffins in an oven.

One says, "Sure is hot in here!"

The other one says, "Holy smokes! A talking muffin!"

What's orange and sounds like a parrot?

A carrot.

What do you get if you cross a cat with an elephant?

A flat cat.

What do you get if you cross a football player with a pay phone?

A wide receiver.

What do you get when you cross a hamburger with a computer?

A big mac!

What do you get when you cross an elephant with a witch?

I don't know but she will need a very large broom!

What do you get when you cross a Border Collie and a daisy?

Cauliflower!

What kind of bagel can fly?

A plain bagel.

Why did the opera singer go sailing?

Because she wanted to hit the high C's.

How does the ocean say hello?

It waves.

How do barbers speed up their jobs?

They make short cuts.

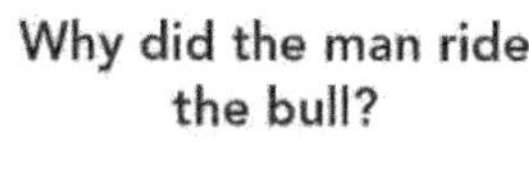

What did Tennessee?

The same thing Arkansas.

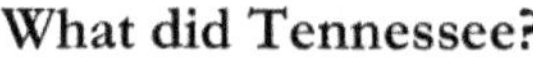

What do you call a story about a broken pencil?

Pointless.

How do you serve a smart hamburger?

On an honor roll.

Where do cars get the most flat tires?

At forks in the road.

What do you call a blind dinosaur?

A Do-you-think-he-saur-us.

How many boos can you put into an empty backpack?

One—after that it isn't empty.

What goes up but never comes down?

Your age.

How many months have 28 days?

All of them.

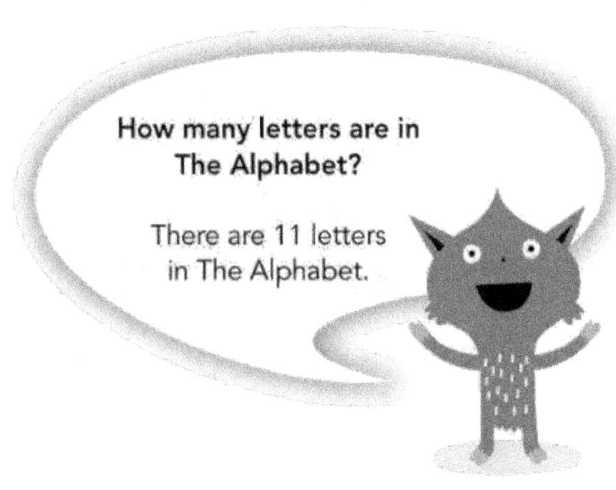

Waiter, will my pizza be long?

No sir, it will be round.

What is black, white, green, and bumpy?

A pickle wearing a tuxedo.

What do you call candy that's been stolen?

Hot chocolate.

How do you make a walnut laugh?

Crack it up.

Which weighs more, a ton of feathers or a ton of bricks?

Neither—they both weigh a ton.

How do you make a milk shake?

Give it a good scare.

What do you get when you cross a porcupine and a turtle?

A slowpoke.

What do you get when you cross a potato with
an elephant?

Mashed potatoes!

What do you get when you cross a mouse with
a squid?

An eektopus!

What is a pretzel's favorite dance?

The twist.

Why do ducks have flat feet?

To stamp out forest fires.

Where does the president keep his armies?

Up his sleevies.

A boy asks his father, "Dad, are bugs good to eat?"

"That's disgusting—don't talk about things like that over dinner," the dad replies.

After dinner the father asks, "Now, son, what did you want to ask me?"

"Oh, nothing," the boy says. "There was a bug in your soup, but now it's gone."

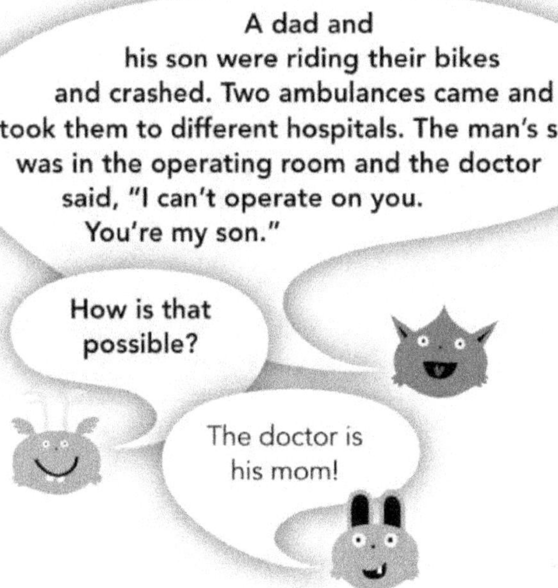

What did one eye say to the other eye?

Don't look now but something between us smells.

What goes up when rain comes down?

An umbrella!

What is the longest word in the dictionary?

Smiles, because there is a mile between the s's.

Throw away the outside and cook the inside, then eat the outside and throw away the inside. What is it?

Corn on the cob, because you throw away the husk, cook and eat the kernels, and throw away the cob.

What has a foot but no legs?

A snail.

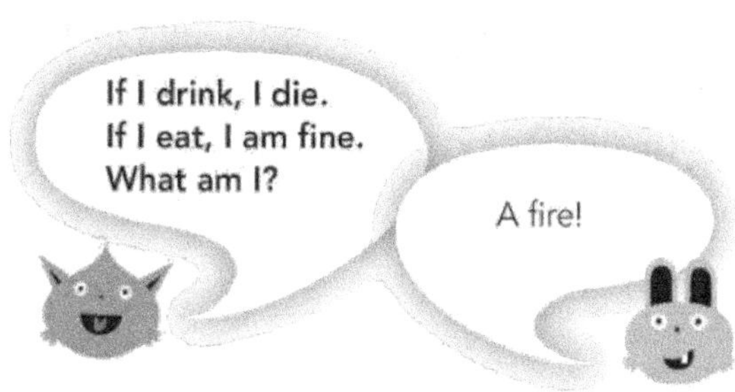

Poor people have it. Rich people need it. If you eat it you die. What is it?

Nothing.

What comes down but never goes up?

Rain.

Mr. Blue lives in the blue house, Mr. Pink lives in the pink house, and Mr. Brown lives in the brown house. Who lives in the white house?

The president!

They come out at night without being called, and are lost in the day without being stolen. What are they?

Stars.

How do you make the number one disappear?

Add the letter G and it's "GONE"

What goes up but never comes down?

Your age!

What starts with the letter "t", is filled with "t", and ends in "t"?

A teapot!

What is so delicate that saying its name breaks it?

Silence.